Sharp Series

Coding with Scratch 3.0 Beta Workbook 1

**Conceptual Learning
An Absolute Beginner's
Visual Guide to Coding**

Lex Sharp

Fields of Code Inc.
Calgary, Alberta
www.fieldsofcode.ca

Copyright © 2018 Fields of Code Inc. All Rights Reserved.

Published by Lex Sharp
Fields of Code Inc.
Calgary, Alberta
Canada
www.fieldsofcode.ca

No part of this publication may be reproduced in any form or by any means, including scanning, photocopying, or otherwise without prior permission of the copyright holder.

ISBN: 978-1-719-876803

FIRST EDITION

THIS BOOK BELONGS TO

_____

Table of Contents

In This Booklet..1
Pre-requisites 1
    Operating Systems 1
    Browsers 2
    Assumptions...2
    Where Is the Browser Address Bar?..3
    Opening a New Tab in a Browser 5
    Installing a Different Browser...6
The Scratch Website 9
    The Latest Version of Scratch: 3.0 9
Your First Project..11
    Adding a Sprite...12
    Selecting a Sprite..14
    Deleting a Sprite...15
Scripts Area 17
    Script Categories 18
    Adding Script Blocks 20
    Removing Script Blocks 20
Coding for the Right Arrow Key..21
    Events...22
    Dragging a Group of Blocks 24
Running the Program 25
On Restart Program 28
    Knowing the Go Button Was Pressed...28

Which Script Group Is Running Currently? 31

    Testing a Group of Blocks on Purpose 32

Coding for the Left Arrow Key 34

Coding the Up and Down Arrow Keys 38

Save, or Rather Download Your Project 41

Review Questions, Test Your Understanding 45

Errata and Feedback 48

Other Books in This Series 49

Coding with Scratch 3.0, Workbook 1

In This Booklet…

The workbooks in this series were meant to be completed in order. This first booklet introduces the student to basic concepts and helps getting started. It covers the following topics:

- verifying and installing the correct Internet browser for Scratch 3.0,
- what is a Sprite,
- identifying the Scratch Stage and Scripts Area,
- adding and removing sprites to the program,
- identifying the currently selected sprite,
- programming the keyboard's arrow-keys for a sprite,
- learn basic computing terms: default, script, command, event, user input, key, running a program, restarting the program,
- using events,
- how blocks react to drag and drop,
- gluing blocks together and dragging them apart,
- learn coding slang: running, dormant code,
- testing a script (glowing blocks),
- using the Windows File Explorer,
- how to save a project onto your computer,
- how Scratch project files are named.

Each booklet takes a bite-sized approach to avoid overwhelming the student.

Pre-requisites

Operating Systems

Our team used Windows 10 in the production of this book, thus all screenshots and results reflect the Windows 10 appearance.

Since Scratch can run in an Internet browser, it does not depend as much on the Operating System as traditional systems do. It is not expected that running in a different operating system would make a difference. The Scratch interface is expected to endure across platforms and more importantly across browsers. The latest version 3.0, of MIT Scratch has been released in January 2019.

Browsers

The new 3.0 version can run on several browsers, for example:

- Chrome
- Opera
- Firefox
- Microsoft Edge

Assumptions

The author assumes the reader has only a basic understanding of

- how Internet browsers work,
- use of the keyboard and mouse (dragging, clicking, etc.),
- basic use of **File Explorer** and navigating to look for a file on the hard drive.

It also helps to know how to use a search engine in the case a different browser needs to be installed.

Regardless of the systems and browsers used, a bit of help follows. If you are already familiar with how to search and browse, skip the parts you already know.

No previous knowledge of coding is required to understand this book series.

Where Is the Browser Address Bar?

To go anywhere online you must use the browser's address bar.

The words **hyperlink, link**, and **address** mean the same thing: a place online.

When you give your browser a hyperlink in the address bar, the browser goes there. The address bar is simply the box in which you type hyperlinks. The address bar is marked by a colored rectangle for each browser as follows.

Chrome:

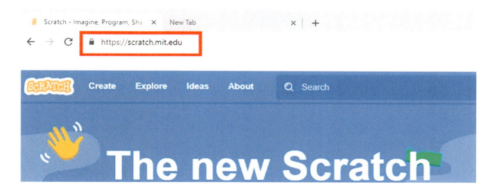

Opera:

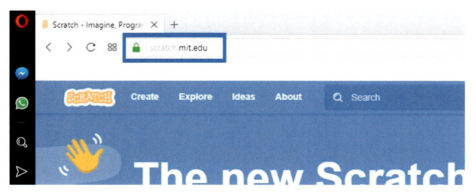

Microsoft Edge:

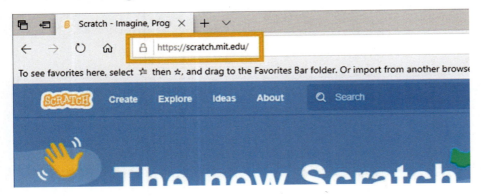

Student Area: Circle your answer.		
I already knew where the address bar is located and how to use it.	YES	NO
I am comfortable using an Internet Browser[1]	YES	NO

---

[1] The answers on this page are meant to help the teacher spot the NO-s quickly and identify such students as needing a bit more support.

Opening a New Tab in a Browser

It's good to keep the things currently worked on in their own browser tabs. When visiting one more website temporarily, it's best to open a new tab which can then be closed when finished. This way there is no disturbing the first work space. To open a new tab, click where the arrows are pointing below. Select your browser from the ones listed.

If your browser looks different, you will need to install the latest version instead to make sure everything works smoothly with no bugs.

Chrome:

Opera:

Microsoft Edge:

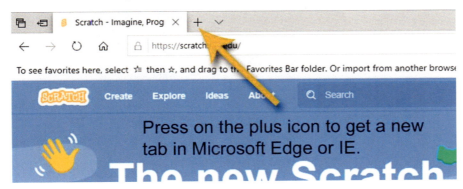

Student Area: Circle your answer.		
I already knew how to open a new tab in my browser.	YES	NO

Installing a Different Browser

First find out what browser are you using, that is what is already installed on your computer before you start.

Student Area: Write it down!		
The name of the browser that is already installed on my computer is	_____.	
Circle your answer: **is your browser** one of the listed in the _Browsers_ section of this chapter on page _2_?	YES	NO

If you have answered **Yes**, you are good to go with that browser and skip to the next chapter from here.

If you have answered **No**, then you must install one of the required browsers instead, so that the Scratch program can work.

Student Area: Ask yourself...		
Am I allowed to install a new browser on my own? Circle your answer.	YES	NO

If you answered **No**:

    Ask a grownup to help you install the right browser for this project.

If you answered **Yes**, continue below.

Coding with Scratch 3.0, Workbook 1

- Open any browser you already have on your computer. You are about to get online and grab the version you want.

- Decide which browser you want to get from the list shown in the <u>Browsers</u> section of this chapter, on page <u>2</u>.

Student Area: Circle the name of the browser you wish to install.		
Chrome	Microsoft Edge	Firefox

- Type the **name of the browser** you circled above in the address bar followed by the word **download**. For example, **Chrome** was used here.
Next, press the **Enter key** at the end of that sentence.

- The results show the words **Download Now**, as seen in the next image, or just plainly the word **download** in the form of a hyperlink. The results will depend on the browser you have chosen.

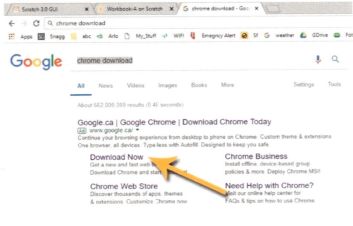

7

- Click on the Download hyperlink shown and follow the instructions given on the screen for that Browser as given.

Student Area: Circle your answer.		
The browser was difficult to install.	YES	NO
Write down the name of the browser that you have installed above.		

The Scratch Website

Let's navigate to the Scratch website, and from there we'll find the new 3.0 version.

Step 1

Open a new tab in your browser. If you're not sure how, see the earlier "*Opening a New Tab in a Browser*" section on page *5*.

Step 2

Place the cursor in the address bar and type:

https://scratch.mit.edu

followed by the Enter key.

The Latest Version of Scratch: 3.0

Version 3.0 was released by the MIT team on January 2019. The first screen is the welcome screen, and it is similar to previous versions. Here is what it looked like when I visited it.

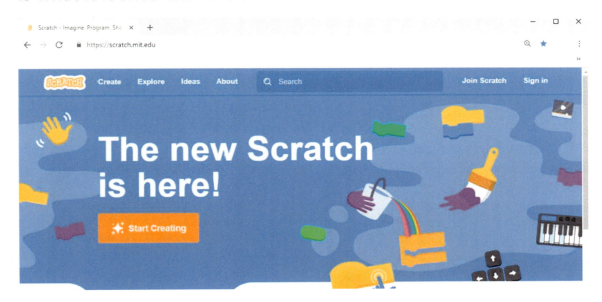

By the time you read this book, your welcome screen may look a bit different, but the main menus and what the program can do will stay the same or similar. As with all online apps, they are dynamic, and will change from time to time, but you will be able to find your way around easily.

Scratch gives you the option for creating an account, but it is not required. Let's dive right in for now and begin coding. We'll learn more about creating accounts in Workbook 5 which is an optional volume.

Press the mouse over the **Create** entry at the top of the screen (see red arrow below).

The main view of the 3.0 version loads and is ready for use. Press the mouse over the x icon at the **Close** menu (see orange arrow below) of any suggested videos. You can watch those another time.

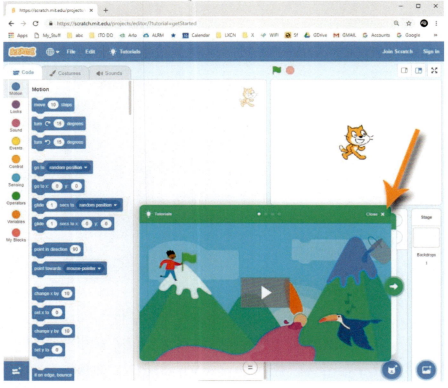

Your First Project

Whenever you type the Scratch hyperlink in your browser's address bar:

https://scratch.mit.edu, you are sure to arrive at the latest version of Scratch. That is currently **version 3.0**.

Asking for an empty project is done by either reloading the web page, or by pressing the **File New** link at the top of the page.

Make sure you do not reload the Scratch page in the browser while you are working on a project. Pressing the Enter key in the address bar will also reload the page. Reloading will take you back to the welcome screen and you will lose all the changes you have made so far.

The first task for this project is to add two characters. One of them will do nothing initially, and the second one will move left, right, up and down when the keyboard arrows are pressed. We'll program the second one later in a different workbook.

Characters in Scratch are called **Sprites**. You will see this term a lot in the program, so try to remember it.

Take a look on at the page at how the Scratch screen is divided up initially and where elements reside.

For every new project, the system gives one Sprite at the beginning, the Cat (see red arrow in the next image). It always appears in the same section of the screen, called the **Stage**.

At the bottom of the screen there is a small box (where the orange arrow points) that controls the sprite.

The other parts of the screen relate to coding.

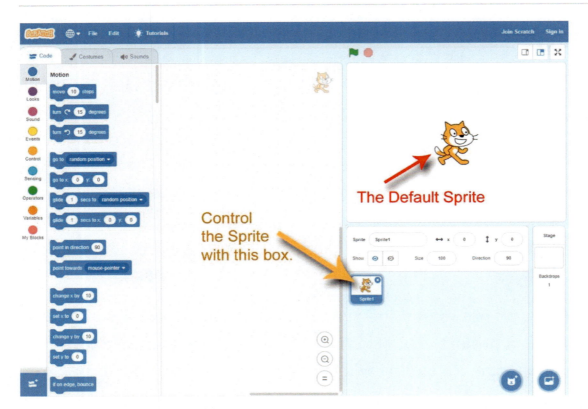

For this project, we'll use a different sprite so that you can learn how to select one, and how to delete the existing cat sprite.

Coding Slang:

What is a **Default**?

A default is something given to you without having to ask for it.

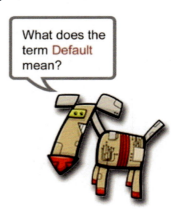

In this example, you can ask for your own sprite, but the default the system gives you without asking is always the Cat sprite at the beginning of each project.

Before we delete the current cat-sprite let's add a couple of new sprites first.

Adding a Sprite

Click the icon shown by the arrow at the bottom right side of the screen.

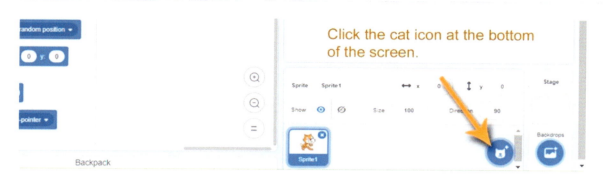

Next, a window shows all the possible sprites you could choose from. Notice at the top of this screen there are categories. At the beginning, the **All** category is selected by default, so everything is listed.

Click on the **Fantasy** category and then find the **Gobo** character. You can choose a different one but selecting the same as this example will make it easier to follow along.

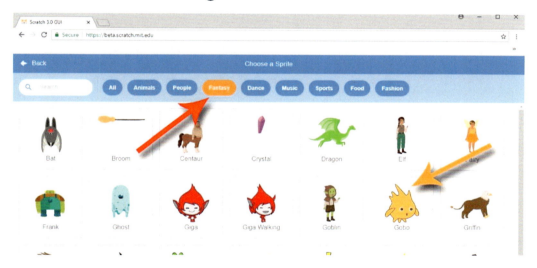

Repeat the process, select the same icon at the bottom of the screen as before, and then pick the **Fantasy** category once more. This time click the mouse in the **Giga Walking** character's square to select it. Notice its name before you click on it. The red-haired sprite is shown below after the selection. This concludes the sprite selection and you are returned automatically to the main page.

13

All the sprites included in this project are shown in the upper right part of the view. A red arrow was added to the image to help you be sure. This part of the screen is called the **Stage**.

Use your mouse to drag the sprites into different positions on the stage, so they are not too crowded.

Control boxes are shown on the right bottom part of this view.

Selecting a Sprite

Check out the pane containing the sprite control boxes in the previous image. This pane appears at the bottom right side of your browser.

Two yellow arrows were added to show the two sprites that we are going to keep for this project.

The blue outline around one of these boxes tells you which the currently selected sprite is. In this view, that box belongs to the **Giga Walking** sprite.

There can be only one selected sprite at a time. Selecting a new sprite removes the selection from the currently selected one.

To change your selection to that of the **Gobo** sprite, click the mouse over its control box. Notice the blue outline is moved to **Gobo**'s box as a result. Gobo's blue frame selection is shown next.

It is important to notice that sprites can also be selected from the Stage by double clicking the character. Whenever you drag a sprite on the stage to reposition it, it also becomes selected automatically.

Which sprite is currently selected becomes important when adding new code. The new code will only apply to the currently selected sprite and to no other.

Deleting a Sprite

Now that you know how to select a sprite, you'll be able to delete it.

We've added two new sprites: Gobo and Giga Walking. We no longer need the cat sprite, let's delete it now.

In the bottom area, click the mouse over the control box that contains the cat sprite, as shown here. As always, the selection is shown by the blue frame.

Click the x icon at the top of the Cat's control box, where the red arrow points.

The system may ask you if you really meant to delete this sprite, say OK and it will disappear from the project.

You are now left with two sprites: Gobo and Giga Walking. Your control box area should only show these two now.

Student Area: Quick Review, check all the boxes that apply.	
How do you know which the currently selected sprite is?	
The pane containing sprite control boxes are located on the	☐ left side of the screen ☐ middle side of the screen ☐ top right side of the screen ☐ bottom right of the screen
Check the box where a currently selected sprite is shown. Do not check any box if you think its sprite is not selected.	☐ Giga Wal... ☐ Gobo

Scripts Area

Another important part of the screen is the **Scripts Area**. To have access to it, the **Code** tab must be selected (red arrow points to it below), otherwise the Scripts area is not seen.

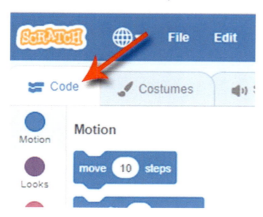

A red rectangle was added around the **Scripts Area** in the image below. It is there only to help you be sure of its position and does not appear in the Scratch program.

The Scripts area is where you will place your code.

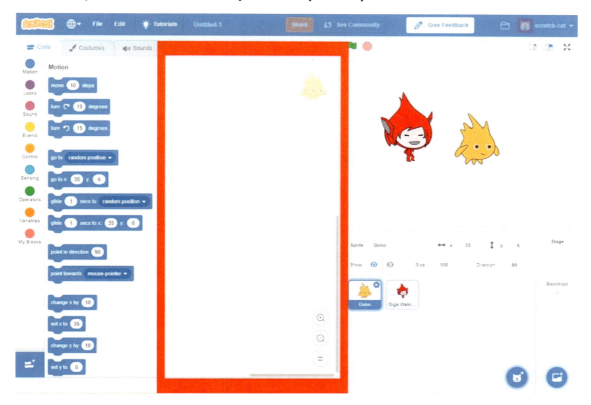

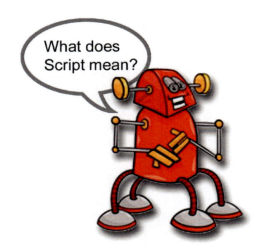

Script is another word for code. It can mean a few lines of code that are easy to activate, or it can also be just one.

Individual lines of code are also known as **commands**.

A **command** is a single instruction that you want the computer to follow. Scratch refers to commands as **Script Blocks**.

An example command is requesting the system to move a sprite 10 points to the right.

A script is made of one or more commands.

Script Categories

Scratch shows all possible code commands graphically in the left side of the screen. A green arrow and rectangle were added in the image below to help you see where this part is.

Different categories of commands are shown. Each category is assigned to a circle, each circle has its own color to help you find what you need faster. Click the mouse over a few of these colored circles to see how the list of commands changes and explore what blocks are available.

The image below shows where the script blocks (or commands) of a chosen category reside on the screen. In this example all script blocks relate to **Motion** (i.e. the blue circle category). The purple rectangle is not part of Scratch, it was added to help you easily spot the area.

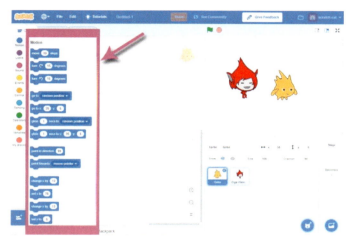

You have now seen the elements of the **Code** tab in the **Script Editor**. Let's review visually where most things are since we'll refer to these terms a lot as we go. This will help you remember.

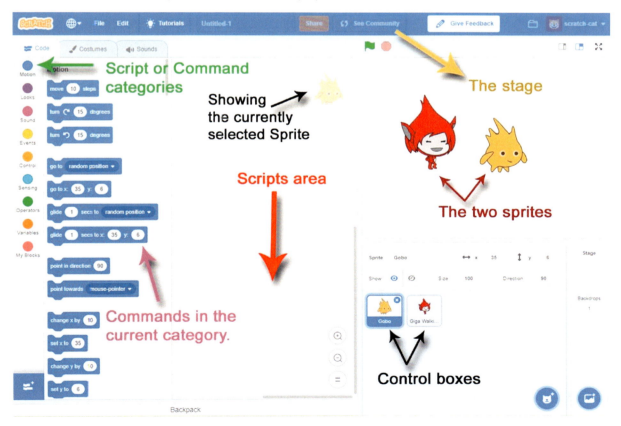

Adding Script Blocks

Coding in Scratch happens by selecting a sprite and then dragging various commands from any category into the **Scripts Area**. There, scripts can be arranged and repositioned as wanted.

A group of commands that are part of the same script, or same idea, can be clumped together in one group by dragging them very close to one another until they glue together. We'll explore this feature further in just a moment.

Removing Script Blocks

If you have moved a command onto the Scripts area and you have changed your mind or it was a mistake, you can get rid of it by dragging it off the Scripts area towards the left side of the screen as shown by the arrows below. This action will remove the command completely from your code.

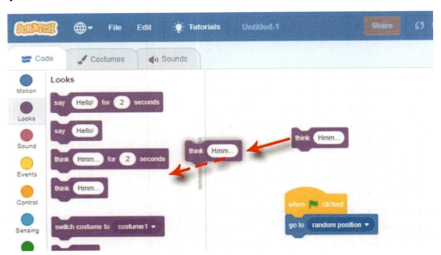

Clicking the mouse accurately, dragging and dropping, are skills that can only be accomplished through practice. In time you will be very comfortable doing so.

Practice adding and removing commands to and from the Scripting area now, before you start adding meaningful code.

Coding for the Right Arrow Key

So far, this project does nothing other than containing the two sprites on the stage and is ready to receive a bit of coding.

Let's start by making one of the sprites move towards the right side of the screen. But we don't want the character to move unless the right arrow key was pressed.

First select the **Giga** sprite by clicking the mouse over its control box.

You want to make sure the correct sprite receives your code.

Knowing the **Right Arrow Key** was pressed on the keyboard depends on recognizing that a keyboard **Event** has occurred.

An **Event** is usually something that happened in the program because the user completed an action. Such is the pressing of a key on the keyboard.

When does this event happen? Whenever the user choses to press a key.

The difference between **events** and commands will become more and more clear as you practice coding. Commands happen when their turn is up, but **events** are caused by someone, or something outside the program and can be out of turn. This can be a user such as yourself, or some other program. User is just another word for player, or person using the game you coded.

Whenever the user does something to use the program that action is also known as: **User Input**.

The system will let your code know an event happened, but it cannot necessarily control when it did.

21

For example, if a user wanted to wait a long time between two key strokes, Scratch can do nothing about that, the user can wait as much as wanted. Additionally, Scratch cannot know in advance which of several possible arrow keys will end up being pressed by the player. Any unexpected keys that were not coded, the game will not react to, leaving the player with no response to those actions.

Events

The Scratch system is well prepared for many events. Click the orange circle in the categories section, it is called **Events**. This will list all event blocks that are available (see red rectangle below). If you scroll down too far, you will stumble on the next category that follows immediately after this selection.

Take a look at the possible events listed. Does any block look like it is related to what is happening on the keyboard?

Notice the event with the "**When … key pressed**" text, shown below.

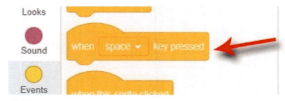

Hold down the left mouse button then drag and drop this block onto the **Scripts** Area.

The block already has a *default* key it handles, but you can choose your own. Initially, or rather the default key in my case was the **Spacebar** key.

On this block there is a tiny white arrow alongside the word **space**. Press it to get a drop down and you'll have several keys to choose from.

The goal is to code in movement for when the **Right Arrow** key is pressed.

Click the mouse over the "**right arrow**" entry so it gets selected. Remember this is just another way to say the user pressed a key.

The event will now say "**when right arrow key pressed**" instead of space.

This part is enough to recognize that a keyboard event occurred. It is our job to decide what should happen in connection to this right arrow event. Next, we'll decide how to react to the key pressed event.

If the right arrow was pressed, the sprite's position should be changed a few points to the right, this will make the sprite look like it has moved a step or two. Don't forget which sprite should be selected: we are doing this for the **Giga** sprite. Make sure you check once in a while the correct sprite is still the one that has the current selection.

Since we want movement, take a look at the **Motion** category. Click on the blue **Motion** circle now. One of the options there is the **move** command. This block ensures the sprite moves in whatever direction the sprite is pointing.

Drag the block onto the **Scripts** area using your mouse. Make sure you position it close to the event. Drag it approaching from below the event block and glue the two together. See an example of how they should look like below on the right.

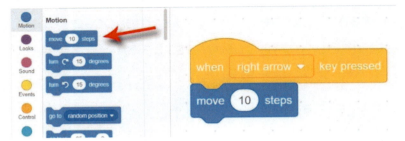

You probably noticed as you dragged closer, a shadow appears below the event block that glues the two to each other. You can now move them as one unit from here on.

To get the Sprite to move more steps, increase the number inside the block, and to move less, reduce it. I'll leave mine as 10 steps because I like how much Giga moves with one press of the arrow key.

It looks like we are finished programming the **Right Arrow Key** for Giga.

Dragging a Group of Blocks

When dragging a block, you can start the dragging action over several areas of the block. Different areas do different things as explained in the next image.

Practice dragging blocks together and apart.

Experiment with where you should begin your dragging. Try detaching the blue block from the event and then gluing it back on again.

Running the Program

Let's run the program and see how it behaves.

There are two ways to run a program in Scratch:

- **Option 1**: in full view so the code editor is not visible, and the program can use a larger part of the screen,
- **Option 2**: inside the code editor by pressing the green flag button to begin (also known as the **Go** button), and the red octagon button to stop.

Let's use **Option 1** for now.

First, notice the three controls at the top right side of the screen.

Notice the rightmost icon, the arrow points at it. Click the mouse over it.

The following screen appears.

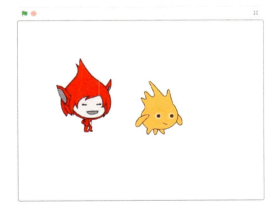

Press the right arrow key on the keyboard to see Giga move to the right. Every time you press the key, the sprite is moved towards the right by 10 points. This is as requested by the **Move** command that you have glued on to the "**when right arrow key pressed**" event earlier.

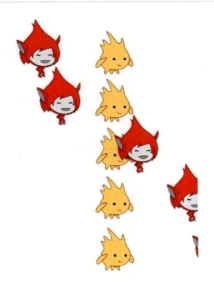

The image on the left shows a new position for Giga on each line, after pressing the right arrow key several times.

If you keep pressing the right arrow key continuously, eventually Giga arrives at the rightmost side of the screen, as shown in the last line of this image.

It then gets stuck there and stops reacting no matter how many times the right arrow is pressed.

This happens because there is no coding to allow the sprite to do anything else but move right. Since the program has run out of Stage space Giga cannot go further.

We'll have to code in Giga's ability to return to the other side of the screen using the left arrow key later.

To stop running the program with **Option 1**, press the icon at the right top corner shown here.

This will take you back to the previous screen.

What Happened to Giga's Position?

Now that the program has stopped running, you will notice the position of Giga on the stage remains at the edge of the screen (see the red arrow in the next image). This is the last position Giga had after the previous run.

Just because you stopped running the program, things are not returned to what they were before you began.

No mess is cleaned up automatically, you will have to take care of this in your code.

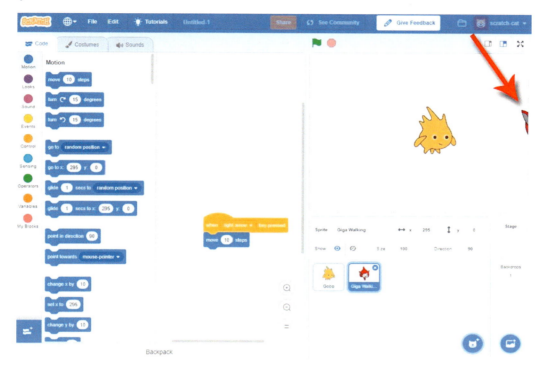

If you want to fix it, you could reposition Giga every time you restart the program. Although, this will not help with the position of Giga at the end of the program, only at the beginning. That is, you will see the cleanup only after you start playing again, not before that.

The following section explains how to code this.

On Restart Program

In Scratch it seems like the program is always running. Nevertheless, the proper way to start of the program is to have the player press the green flag player. This is often referred to as a program **start** or **restart**.

The green flag button is also called the **Go** button.

The red octagon button on the right side of the green flag is the **Stop** button and ends the current run.

If you pressed the **Go** button without leaving the editor you are then running the program with **Option 2** mentioned in the *Running the Program* chapter on page *25*.

Knowing the Go Button Was Pressed

You can ask the system to tell your game when the **Go** button was pushed. Consider the player's button-pressing action to be an **event**.

This is done through the "**when green flag clicked**" script block shown below. Drag it with your mouse from the **Events** category onto the **Scripts** area. For this you will have to first press the Yellow circle to get the list of all scripts in this category.

Let's code in a repositioning of Giga with this event.

First hover the mouse above the Stage. There drag Giga into the position where you want it to appear at the moment the program restarts. Remember, the restart only happens after the player pushes the green flag button.

In this example I have dragged Giga to the lower left corner of the Stage. That's the position I have chosen for Giga to be in at the beginning of my game.

Observe the control area below the Stage. The x and y coordinates track the exact position of Giga (see blue arrows). below.

These numbers update whenever the sprite is moved.

Try repositioning several times and watch the numbers in the **x** and **y** boxes change. Make sure the Giga sprite remains selected.

Next, choose the blue circle for the **Motion** category of scripts.

There are two blocks in this category that begin with the words "**go to**".

29

Of these two, find the "**go to**" script that has an **x** and **y** in it: "**go to x: … y: …**". Drag it onto the Scripts area below the "**when green flag clicked**" block. Bring it close enough to glue them together. See how the two should looks like below.

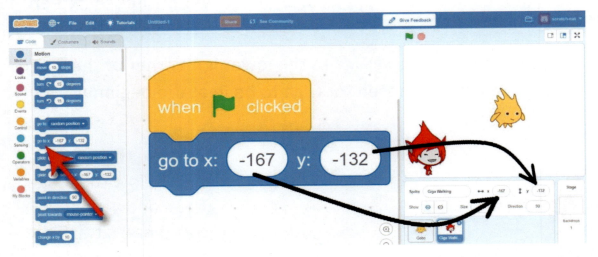

We have just positioned Giga at the left corner of the Stage a moment ago. When dragging the "**go to x: … y: …**" block on to the Scripts area, it picked up the current **x** and **y** Giga had at that time. You can compare the block values and those in the control box as suggested by the two black arrows shown above.

After gluing the two blocks, they belong and act together from there on.

Let's use **Option 2** described earlier to run the program inside the code editor.

Press the **Go** button, then press the right arrow key repeatedly and watch Giga move to the right until the edge of the Stage area is reached.

Press the **Go** button again to restart the game. In that moment you should see Giga jump back to the lower left corner of the Stage as instructed by the code you've just added.

You are now finished coding the "**when green flag clicked**" event.

Which Script Group Is Running Currently?

There can be many blocks in a code. When you start the program, most blocks remain dormant[2] while other block groups are actively doing something. There can be many groups activating at the same time.

Groups take turns and become dormant or active based on what is happening in the moment. For example, if a Scratch program has 6 script groups that have a "**when green flag clicked**" block at the top of each, then all the 6 groups will awaken when the player presses the Go button.

Instead of saying the block is active you can also say the block is "**running**".

Prepare to run the program using **Option 2**, from inside the script editor.

Our game only has two script groups so far. Let's observe them in the Scripts area. An arrow was added on the side of each group to highlight the location.

In this example, each group is made of two blocks: one yellow, and one blue.

---

[2] Dormant means asleep. When it's about code, dormant means code that is not being used right now.

Press the **Go** button.

Make sure you keep your eyes on the Scripts area and its blocks while you press down and hold the right arrow key at the same time.

You should see only the group that handles the arrow key glowing. The glow looks like this, it has a yellow halo. The second group should not have a halo at this time.

The glowing stops when the player stops pressing the arrow key.

This feature is there to show which groups of blocks was awakened by your actions. In other words which group is **running**.

The second group of blocks, (pointed in the earlier image by the purple arrow) was not affected. That group handles the green flag event only and has nothing to do with arrow keys. It didn't need to activate, it is not glowing. This shows you that it is asleep for now.

To experiment with this feature further, again while keeping your eyes on the Scripts area push down on the Go button repeatedly and see the second group of blocks activates with a glow instead.

The groups that glow are the only ones doing something in the moment.

Testing a Group of Blocks on Purpose

Try this out: let's say you want to test the group of blocks that moves Giga to the right.

Go to the Scripts area where the blocks are and click the mouse button over the group with the right arrow event.

Make sure you click the mouse repeatedly over the area where the red arrow is pointing, as shown above.

Every time the mouse is clicked, the sprite on the Stage area makes a movement to the right. This happens without the user having to press the **right arrow** key on the keyboard, or the Go button, because you are activating the **testing feature**.

The testing feature offers you a simple way to check that your bundle of blocks is doing its job as you imagined them to, without having to run the entire game first.

Coding for the Left Arrow Key

It's time to help Giga react to the **left arrow**.

Let's copy the ideas from the **right arrow** coded earlier.

All that needs to be changed are:

- the key handled should now be the **left** arrow instead of the **right**,
- movement should happen towards the **left** rather than **right**.

Make sure that Giga is the selected sprite.

Go to the **Events** category (the yellow circle) and drag a new "**when … key pressed**" block onto the Scripts area.

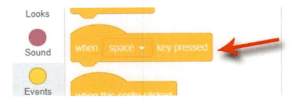

Like before, use the tiny white arrow on this block to open the drop down and select the **left arrow** entry (shown below).

Go to the **Motion** category (the blue circle) and drag in a **Move** script block.

Bring it as close as possible to the event block to glue the two together.

Notice the default movement for this block is **10 steps**.

You probably noticed earlier that for every right key stroke the position of Giga was moved 10 points. The movement happens in whatever **direction** Giga is pointing to.

The image below shows where the **direction** box is (see red arrow).

In this example, Giga has a 90° direction. When you click in the direction box, initially the number 90 is shown. A helpful circle appears with a white arrow that translates the degrees' meaning into a direction that can be visualized.

The movement will happen in the direction the white arrow points. You can see the movement in this image would be straight forward to the right, which is where the white arrow is pointing.

Drag the white arrow around in the circle and notice how that changes the direction of the sprite. See the degrees number change as well.

Remember to test your program by running it before you decide to keep your changes.

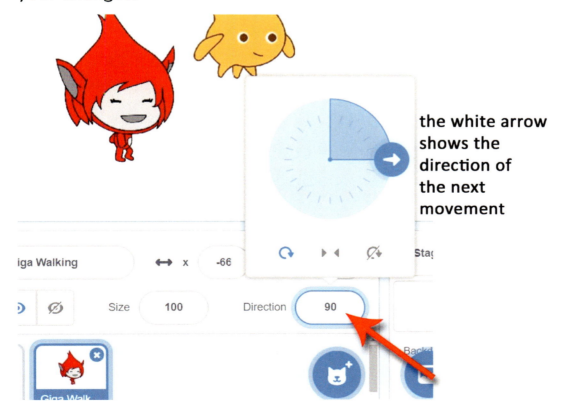

the white arrow shows the direction of the next movement

Let's stop for a moment and think about the code we added earlier for the **right** arrow. We had a movement towards the right side of the screen 10 points at a time for every key stroke.

It is important to notice the points, or rather the number were **positive**. This worked just like the number line

- in math, **positive** steps go to the **right**, and
- **negative** steps would move in the opposite direction to the **left**.

The positive direction looks like this.

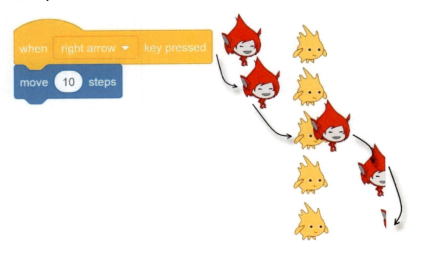

It should be easy to guess that by changing the positive to negative (using the minus sign) we could get movement in the opposite direction, that is to the left.

We've just added a left arrow key event on page _34_, also seen in the next image. You must fix the number in the blue move box. It may say 10, or some other number for now.

To do this click the mouse inside the block's white bubble (see an arrow pointing to it next).

Type the number **-10** in to replace whatever number you have in your box.

Next time you press the left arrow you should see movement to the left as shown in the next progression.

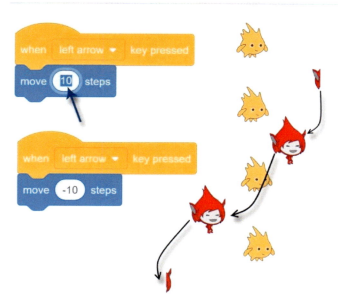

This completes the programming of the **left arrow** key.

Coding the Up and Down Arrow Keys

Handling the up and down movement is very similar to the way we have coded the left and right arrows.

Up requires the addition of positive steps and down that of negative steps. We just have to make sure we work on the vertical movement rather than the horizontal.

Notice that the earlier **move block** we used will only cause movements in the direction that Giga is pointing. Direction is based on the degrees you have given.

Instead, movement can be forced to happen in the horizontal or vertical line, regardless of direction.

For each type of movement, horizontal and vertical, there is a separate block:

- **horizontal**: "**change x by**", and
- **vertical**: "**change y by**" script block.

The two blocks look like this.

Horizontal   Vertical

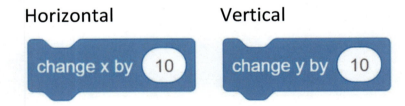

Both blocks can be found in the **Motion** category (the blue circle).

Notice the x and y in the wording.

Control the left and right as follows:

- **positive** x represents movement to the **right,** and
- **negative** x takes movement to the **left**.

Similarly, control the up and down so

- **positive** y represents movement to the **up,** and
- **negative** y takes movement down.

Then let's hook up this new block to the up and down key events, which is how we know that the player pressed a key.

Make sure Giga is selected before you begin.

Select the **Events** category.

Drag two **key events** onto the Scripts area. That is, you drag and drop the same event twice as shown below. We'll use one for the down and the other for the up.

Change each of the block's default keys. Here, they show **space** first, and we don't want that. For the first block, select the **up arrow**, and for the second block select the **down arrow**. Your blocks should look like shown next.

Drag in one "**change y by …**" block for each of the two yellow events. Glue each by dragging it closer as shown in the image below.

The group on the left handles the **arrow up**, it will work well because positive steps of y create movement upwards. We can leave a positive value of 10 in that box.

In this example, the group on the right that handles the **down arrow** does the same, also moves upwards. It must be fixed to move downwards by using negative steps instead.

Click the mouse inside the white number bubble on the **down arrow** group and type **-10** instead of 10 (see image on the right).

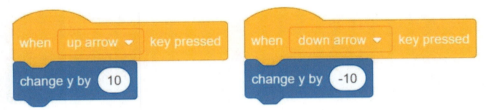

You are now ready to run the code again.

Press the green Go flag and use every arrow key to check that the movement of Giga is correct. Then press the green flag when you want Giga to jump back to its starting position, for me that was the left bottom of the screen.

You have now completed the programming of the **Up** and **Down** arrow keys for Giga.

Save, or Rather Download Your Project

Seems like you have done enough coding on this project that it's time to save the changes.

Since for now you are using Scratch without logging[3] into an account, the save project option is not applicable. Instead you can **download** any project onto your computer, and next time you return to Scratch you can upload it back again just before you start coding.

Remember to do this again whenever you have completed a task, so you always have a copy of your latest changes.

Your screen will look similar to this.

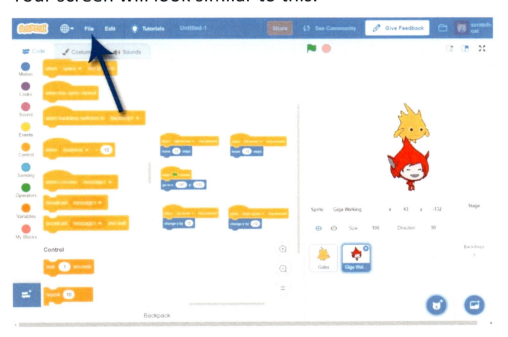

Notice the arrow points to the main menu where the **File** entry is.

Click on the **File** entry now.

Next, a pop-up menu appears as shown in the next image.

---

[3] Tip for Teachers: Creating Scratch accounts is covered in the optional Workbook 5. There is no point to learn this until the students have covered enough ground and it's clear they like coding. We'll focus on coding in the first four workbooks, as the lack of an account is not an impediment.

Choose the **Save to your computer** entry.

This will initiate a full download of the project into your default **Downloads** folder.

The **Downloads** folder is where your Internet Browser typically puts files you decide to download onto your computer.

The Scratch system will not give you a chance to rename the download, but you can use the **Windows File Explorer** later to do so when finished. Although you might decide you don't need to.

The completed download is indicated in the left bottom side of your browser, by the name of the file, as shown by the red arrow below.

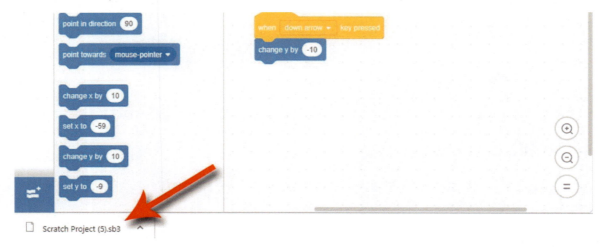

Once the download is finished, you can navigate to the **Downloads** folder using your Windows File Explorer to verify the file is really there.

The yellow arrow below shows you the **File Explorer address bar**. There you can choose the **"This PC"** option and click on the **Downloads** folder from underneath it. If this is not the first time the project was downloaded it gets a number in brackets side by side with the name to show this happened so many times. In this example, I have done so 5 times so my project was named Scratch Project (5).sb3.

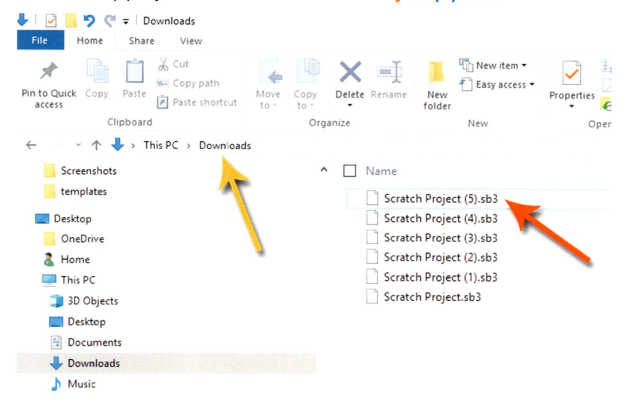

The file names are listed in the file pane area on the right (where the red arrow points).

The name of the file is made of three elements:

- Scratch Project is the text for the name of the project, I left mine as is,
- (5) represents the number of times you have downloaded a project from Scratch,
- the file extension **sb3** has 3 in it to remind you of the current version number of Scratch: **3.0**.

You may want to change the name in the beginning part - for example replace the **Scratch Project** prefix with something meaningful like **giga-walking-project**, or whatever your idea is instead. I am OK with the name given so I'll leave it as is.

Every time you download a project the name will be composed as shown above, and it will always be different because it will have a different number in the brackets. This is good because if you are given a different file name at every download, then files will not overwrite and replace earlier versions of code.

This will help decide which is the latest and the oldest file, and you won't be confused.

This is it for the **Workbook 1**. Try out the review questions at the end of the booklet to test your understating.

Check out **Workbook 2** for how to upload your saved project next time and learn a bunch of new coding skills.

Review Questions, Test Your Understanding

Question 1

There can be only one sprite selected at a time. Which page in this booklet shows how to know which sprite is currently selected?

The answer is page number _____ .

Question 2

Which page in this booklet shows how to delete a sprite?

The answer is page number _____ .

Question 3

Which page in this booklet shows most parts of the Script editor and their names?

The answer is page number _____ .

What is the name of the tab that should be selected at the top to make sure the Script editor is visible?

The name of the tab is _____ .

Question 4

What does the Green Go Flag button do?

Question 5

What does the Red Octagon Flag button do?

_____

_____

Question 6

Which page in this booklet shows how to download your project to your own computer?

The answer is page number _____ .

Question 7

Which page in this booklet shows how to remove a Script block from the Scripts Area?

The answer is page number _____ .

Question 8

In one example in this booklet, we wanted Giga to be repositioned to the left bottom corner of the Stage. This was to happen at the start of every new run.

What was the event used to make this work?

The event has this text on it: _____ .

Question 9

What is the difference between a regular script block and an **Event**?

_____

_____

_____

Question 10

Adding movement steps to a Sprite is like the movement on the number line in Math.

Place the terms: **left, right, up or down** correctly to complete the sentences below.

Positive steps to **x** cause movement towards the _____.

Negative steps to **x** cause movement towards the _____.

Positive steps to **y** cause movement towards the _____.

Negative steps to **y** cause movement towards the _____.

Question 11

The type of block that helps your program recognize a key was pressed is of the color _____, and has the following text on it:

_____.

It can be found in the _____ script category.

Errata and Feedback

What are **Errata**?

Sometimes when authors write their books, even after thorough checks, errors can still make their way into a book.

When an error is discovered after printing, it's good to have a place - for example online - where these errors can be recorded so the reader can be warned.

This is especially important for textbooks and manuals.

The place where such errors can be reported is called **Errata** and means a list of published errors.

You should always check all your textbooks, including this one, for erratas before you begin your learning.

This book's Errata can be found at:

https://sharpseries.ca/scratch/errata1.html

Comments and suggestions for future editions are always welcome.

Other Books in This Series

Find out more about **Workbooks 1 to 4** in this series at: https://sharpseries.ca/scratch/w.html.

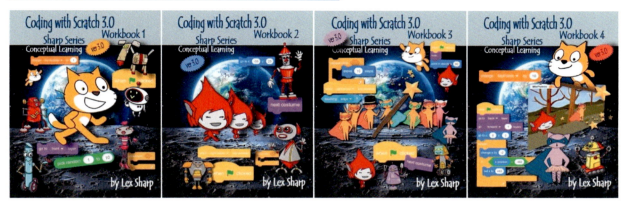

Find out more about **Early Math Concepts** at:

https://sharpseries.ca/em/v1.html.

Find out more about **Chemistry for Kids** at:

https://sharpseries.ca/chem/v1.html.

(All orders are fulfilled by Amazon)

Made in the USA
Middletown, DE
16 January 2019